1 The Story Begins

The story of Jesus began 2000 years ago, in a warm and sunny land. It was home to a people who called themselves the Jews.

In this quiet little world, Jesus became famous as a preacher.

He talked to people about God. He talked about how to live in the way that God wants.

A farmer sows seeds

Shepherds lead their sheep to graze on the hills of Galilee

A potter in his open-air workshop

Carrying water from the well

A woman weaves on the flat roof of her home

I want to
know about
Jesus

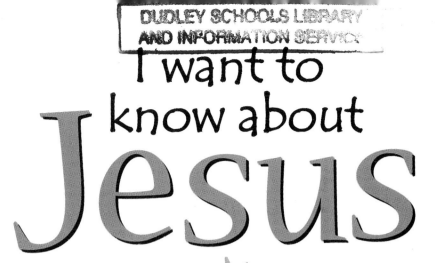

Christina Goodings

Illustrated by
Jan Lewis

LION

Contents

Many people believed what he said and they chose to follow him. They became known as Christians.

Many people in the world today are Christians. They too try to follow Jesus' teaching.

FOUR SPECIAL BOOKS

Four special books tell people about Jesus. They are called the Gospels: the Gospel of Matthew, the Gospel of Mark, the Gospel of Luke and the Gospel of John. They are all in the Christian holy book – the Bible.

Fishermen take their boats out on Lake Galilee to fish

Jesus tells stories to the children

2 Jesus is Born

Here is what the Gospel of Luke says about the birth of Jesus.

One day, the angel Gabriel went to Nazareth. The angel had a message for a young woman named Mary.

'God has chosen you,' said the angel. 'You will be the mother of God's own Son.'

Mary was puzzled, but she agreed to do as God wanted.

Soon, everyone around her knew she was expecting a baby.

Her husband-to-be was Joseph. He still wanted to marry Mary even though the baby wasn't his.

Together they went to Bethlehem to put their names on an important list: the Roman emperor's new list of taxpayers.

The town was crowded. Mary and Joseph had to shelter in a stable. Mary had her baby there.

An angel is a messenger from God

The angel Gabriel

Mary

Joseph

Mary

Baby Jesus

The shepherds have their sheep on the hillside and come to Bethlehem

She wrapped him snugly and used a manger – a feed box for animals – as a cradle.

On the hills nearby, shepherds were watching their sheep. Angels appeared, shining as brightly as heaven. 'God's king has been born in Bethlehem,' they sang.

The shepherds went to see. They found Joseph, Mary and her baby, Jesus. They believed that what the angels had said was true.

CHRISTMAS

Christians remember the stories of Jesus' birth at Christmas, on 25 December. Many Christians make a little display of Jesus' cradle in the stable. This is a nativity scene.

3 Gifts for a Newborn King

Wise priest

Herod

Here is what the Gospel of Matthew says about the birth of Jesus.

In a faraway country, wise and learned men saw a new star. 'It is a sign,' they said, 'that a new king has been born.'

They wanted to worship the king, so they followed the star all the way to the Jewish city of Jerusalem. 'Where is the new king of the Jews?' they asked.

In his palace, King Herod began to fret. He ruled the country from Jerusalem, and didn't want another king! He asked his own wise men for help.

'Listen as we read from our Jewish holy books,' they said. 'One day, God's special king will be born in Bethlehem.'

Herod sent the travelling wise men to the little town. They found Jesus with his mother. They gave him rich gifts.

THREE GIFTS

The wise men gave Jesus three gifts: gold, frankincense and myrrh. These costly gifts were the offering fit for a great king. Because there were three gifts, many people think that there were three wise men.

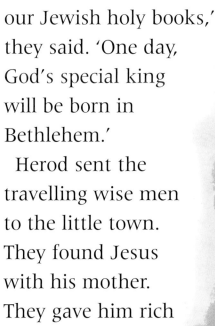

An angel warned the wise men not to go back to Herod. They went home a different way.

An angel warned Joseph to take Mary and Jesus and go to Egypt. They went there and were safe. When Herod died, they went to Nazareth.

Frankincense

The wise men are said to visit Mary and Jesus in a house

Myrrh

Gold

The message of the wise men's visit is this: other nations believed that Jesus was a king

4 Jesus Grows Up

The boy Jesus learns to read the holy books

Jesus was a Jew and he learned the Jewish faith. He learned how to read the holy books. He learned about the Law that had been given to the people long before.

When he was twelve, his parents took him to Jerusalem for the Passover festival. It was celebrated at the Temple there.

Afterwards, everyone from Nazareth set off for home together. It was late in the day when Mary noticed: Jesus wasn't in the crowd!

She and her husband hurried back to find him.

He was in the Temple. He was talking about the Jewish faith with the wise teachers.

'Why did you make us so worried?!' cried Mary.

PASSOVER

Here is the story of the festival for which Jesus went to Jerusalem.

A long, long time before, the people of Israel had been slaves in Egypt.

God had chosen Moses to rescue them.

The night of the escape was called Passover: the night when danger passed over them.

Soon after, God gave Moses laws to guide the people. These great sayings reminded the people to obey God and to do the things that are right and good.

Jesus and all the Jewish people still wanted to obey this Law. As in days of old, God was their God; they were God's people.

The courtyard of the Temple in Jerusalem

Mary and her husband

Jewish teachers are called rabbis

The boy Jesus

Jesus was surprised. 'Didn't you know that I had to be in my Father's house?' he asked.

Then he went home with them. He was a good and obedient son and learned the family trade. People in Nazareth knew him as the carpenter's son.

The teachers listen to Jesus very carefully and are interested to hear what he tells them about the holy books

5 Jesus' New Start

When he was grown up, Jesus made a new start. First, he went to see a holy man named John. 'Please baptize me,' said Jesus. Baptism was a sign of turning to God.

John was surprised: he knew that Jesus had always obeyed God. When he baptized Jesus, he heard a voice from heaven. The voice said that Jesus was God's Son.

The dove is a sign of God's Holy Spirit

Jesus asks to be baptized

John the Baptist is Jesus' cousin

In the wild country, Jesus has nothing to eat

Then Jesus went out into the wild country. He spent forty days thinking and praying about what to do next.

The Devil came to talk to him. 'Are you really God's Son?' whispered the Devil. 'If you are, you could have anything you want. You could make yourself rich and powerful.'

'I won't do that,' said Jesus. 'I've read the holy books. I am going to live as God truly wants.'

BAPTISM

Christians today baptize people who are new to the faith. They do this by dipping people in water. It is a sign that they want to live as a child of God.

6 Jesus the Preacher

Joanna

Mary Magdalene

Susanna

Jesus became a preacher. He began to travel to all the towns and villages near to where he lived. He made his home in a town called Capernaum, on the shore of Lake Galilee.

He told people how to live as God's friends: 'Then you will be part of God's kingdom,' he said.

He said that the kingdom was a bit like a tree: it grew from a tiny seed. It became a place where all the birds could safely nest.

Jesus also worked miracles. He had power from God to make sick people well. People flocked to see him.

JESUS AND HIS HELPERS

Jesus knew he needed people to help him: he needed more people to spread the news about the kingdom of God.

He began by choosing four of the men who fished on Lake Galilee. Then he chose eight more: the twelve were the disciples.

There were women who helped too. Mary Magdalene was someone Jesus had healed. Joanna and Susanna were wealthy. They helped pay for the things Jesus needed.

Simon, Andrew, James and
John were fishermen

James and his brother John

Andrew,
Simon's
brother

Simon, who
was also
called Peter

Judas
Iscariot

Matthew

Philip

Another
Simon

James

Judas

Bartholemew

Thomas

7 The Right Thing to Do

PARABLES

Jesus often told stories to help people understand his teaching. These stories-with-a-message are called parables. The story about the two house-builders is a parable. So is the story about the Samaritan on the next page.

Jesus wanted people to do the things that are right and good.

He told them what that meant.

'Be kind to everyone, even those who are unkind to you.

'Don't just love your friends. Love your enemies too, and say prayers for them.

'Do good in secret. Don't show off when you give to the poor.

'Don't worry about money and buying things. The birds and the flowers don't, and God still takes care of them. God will take care of you.

'Forgive people who do wrong things. Then God will forgive you.

'Listen to what I say,' said Jesus,
'and obey it. Then you will be like the man
who built his house on rock. The rain came,
the flood rose: his house stood safe.
  'If you do not listen and obey, you will be like
the man who built his house on sand. The rain
came, the flood rose: his house fell flat.'

Jesus says that obeying
his teaching is like a
house with good
foundations

8 Old Teaching, New Teaching

Robbers run off with the money

The things Jesus said left some people puzzled.

Was his teaching the same as the old laws of the Jewish people, or was it new?

One day, a teacher of the Law came to Jesus. He wanted to find out if Jesus understood the old laws properly.

'What must I do to be God's friend for ever and ever?' he asked.

'What does our Jewish Law say?' answered Jesus.

'It says that we must love God above all,' said the teacher, 'and we must love other people as much as ourselves.'

'Quite right,' said Jesus.

'But who are these "other people"?' demanded the teacher.

'Listen,' said Jesus. 'Once a man went from Jerusalem to Jericho. Robbers came and beat him up. They left him for dead.

A Temple helper stops to look

A man is robbed

A Temple priest came along. He saw the man lying on the ground but hurried on by.

A helper from the Temple came along. He came closer to look at the man, but then he hurried on by.

'A non-Jew came along – a Samaritan. He saw the man and went to help him. He took him to an inn. He paid for his care.

'Now tell me which of the three showed that he loved others as much as himself.'

'The Samaritan,' said the man.

'Quite right,' said Jesus. 'That's what you should do.'

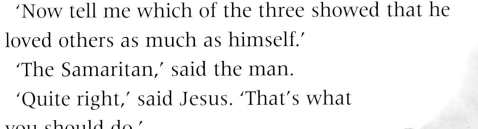

A Temple priest hurries by

A Samaritan stops to help

9 The Right Way to Pray

THE LORD'S PRAYER

The prayer that Jesus taught is called the Lord's Prayer or the Our Father.

For Christians, it is the most important prayer of all. They often say this to end the prayer:

'The kingdom,
the power and
the glory are yours.
Amen.'

Jesus spent time every day praying to God.

'Please teach us to pray,' said his disciples.

'When you pray,' replied Jesus, 'you should do so alone and quietly.

'A short prayer is all you need. Say this:

'Father:
Your name is holy;
May everyone honour you.
May your kingdom come.
May your will be done on earth,
Just as it is in heaven.
Give us day by day the food we need.
Forgive us the wrong we have done,
Just as we forgive the wrong that others have done to us.
Keep us safe from any hard times that might shake our faith and trust in you.

'Ask,' said Jesus, 'and you will receive.
 'Seek, and you will find.
 'Knock, and the door will be opened to you.
 'You already know that loving parents want
to give good things to their children.
 'God is more loving than the best parent.
God will give good things to you.'

10 God's Love

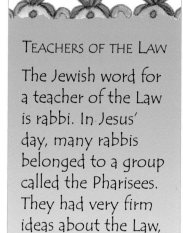
All kinds of people came to listen to Jesus. Some of them knew they had done very wrong things. Others were rather proud about how good they were – especially the teachers of the Law.

Jesus wanted them all to understand what God thinks about those who do wrong.

'Listen,' said Jesus. 'There was once a man who had two sons.

'The younger son didn't want to obey his father. He asked for money and went off far away. He lived foolishly.

'Then the money was gone. He got a job looking after pigs. He sat in the dust with them and felt very sad.

Rabbis

Looking after pigs – a lowly and dirty job

' "I will go back to my father," he said to himself. "I will say I am sorry. I will ask to be a servant on the family farm."

'He walked the long road home. He was still a long way off when his father saw him. His father came running to meet him. He hugged his son and kissed him.

' "We must have a party and be glad," he said. He told the servants to get everything ready.

'The elder son was cross. "Why are you being so kind to that good-for-nothing?" he grumbled. "It's not fair."

' "Please come and join in the party," replied the father. "That good-for-nothing is my son. He was lost, but now we have found him." '

The grumpy older son

The sorrowful younger son

The welcoming father

11 Power to Forgive

One day, Jesus was teaching in someone's house. Many teachers of the Law had come to listen to him.

Others crowded near. In the end, no one could even get to the door!

Some men wanted to bring their friend to Jesus. Their friend could not walk, so his friends were carrying him on his sleeping mat.

When they saw the crowds by the door, they went up the steps to the flat roof.

They made a hole in the roof. Then they lowered their friend right in front of Jesus.

A roof has branches and plaster between the rafters. It is easy to break and fix

Jesus looks up

'Your sins are forgiven, my friend,' said Jesus.
The teachers of the Law began to grumble. 'A person isn't allowed to say that. Only God can forgive sins.'

Jesus looked at them. 'I am going to show you that I am allowed to say that,' he said. He turned to the man. 'Get up off your bed and walk.'

The man got up. By a miracle, he was able to walk. He was overjoyed.

FORGIVING OTHERS

Jesus told his followers that they should forgive people.
'How often?' asked Simon Peter. 'Is seven times enough?'
'Not seven times,' said Jesus, 'but seventy times seven.'

The four friends lower the man who cannot walk

12 Miracles to Change the World

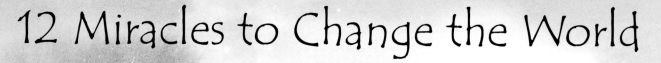

Jesus worked many miracles. They were signs of God's power to change the world.

One day, 5,000 people came to listen to Jesus. They stayed all day, and in the end everyone was hungry.

A young boy offered Jesus' disciples his own food: five loaves of bread and two fish. Jesus took it, said a prayer of thanks, and asked the disciples to share it with the crowd.

By a miracle, it was enough for everyone.

One evening, Jesus and his disciples got on their fishing boat to cross Lake Galilee. Jesus fell asleep. In the night, a storm blew in. The boat began to sink.

'Help us!' cried the disciples, as they shook Jesus awake.

Jesus stood up in the boat. 'Be quiet!' he said to the waves. 'Be still!' he said to the wind.

By a miracle, the lake grew calm.

One day, a man named Jairus came to Jesus.

'Hurry to my house,' he said. 'My little girl is dying.'

Along the way, people crowded close to them. Jesus even stopped to talk. When they reached Jairus' house, the little girl had died.

Jesus went to her bedside. 'Little girl,' he said, 'get up.'

She sat up, alive and well.

13 Jesus and the Children

GUARDIAN ANGELS

Jesus said that a child's angel is always close to God. Because of this, many Christians say that everyone has a guardian angel.

The disciples were happy to be Jesus' closest friends. As more and more people flocked to see Jesus, they began to feel important.

They even began to argue about which of them was the most important.

Jesus asked a child to come and stand in front of them. 'Listen,' he said to the disciples. 'Unless you change and become like this child, you will not be part of the kingdom.

'The greatest person in the kingdom is the one who acts humbly.

Jesus welcomes children

'And if you welcome a child like this in my name, you welcome me.

'Never look down on little ones like these. Each one has an angel in heaven and their angel is always close to God.

'Think of a shepherd who has one hundred sheep. He will leave ninety-nine grazing in the pasture while he goes to look for one which is lost.

'God does not want any of these little ones to be lost.'

Grown-ups and children are important to God

A shepherd rescues his stray sheep

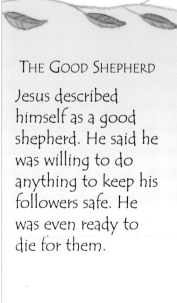

THE GOOD SHEPHERD

Jesus described himself as a good shepherd. He said he was willing to do anything to keep his followers safe. He was even ready to die for them.

14 Who Will Follow Jesus?

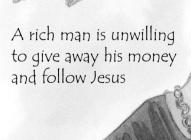

One day, a rich young man came to Jesus.

'What must I do to live as God's friend for ever?' he asked.

'You must keep the laws,' replied Jesus.

'I always have,' said the young man. 'What else can I do?'

'You must sell all you have,' said Jesus. 'Give the money to the poor, then come and follow me.'

The young man went away shaking his head!

'That's very sad,' said Jesus. 'It is hard for rich people to be part of God's kingdom.'

On another day, Jesus went to Jericho. People crowded the streets to see him.

The tax collector in the town was Zacchaeus. He had cheated people to make himself rich.

Zacchaeus was a short man. He wanted to be able to see over the crowds, so he climbed a tree.

Jesus stopped underneath. 'Come down,' he called. 'I want to stay in your house.'

A rich man is unwilling to give away his money and follow Jesus

The crowds laugh to see their tax collector in a tree

Jesus calls Zacchaeus

Zacchaeus wants to get a good look at Jesus

The people of Jericho grumbled. 'Why is Jesus eating with a cheat?' they asked.

Jesus helped Zacchaeus to change his ways. 'I am going to give half of what I own to the poor,' Zacchaeus declared. 'I am going to repay the people I cheated with four times more than I took.'

Jesus was pleased. 'I am here to rescue those who are far away from God,' he said.

TRUE RICHES

Jesus warned his followers not to make money the most important thing in life. Instead, they should set their hearts on doing the things that please God.

15 Jesus Rides to Jerusalem

Jesus was a preacher for about three years.

Another Passover time came.

'I want to be in Jerusalem for the festival,' said Jesus to his disciples. 'I want you to fetch me a donkey so I can ride there.'

Lots of people were going to Jerusalem for the festival. When they saw Jesus riding to the city, some of them began to whisper.

'There's the preacher who talks about the kingdom of God. Perhaps he's about to make himself king in Jerusalem.'

The whisper began to spread. Then someone gave a shout: 'God bless the king! God bless the king.'

Some people threw their cloaks down to carpet the road. Others cut palm branches and waved them like flags.

Palm leaves

Some Pharisees were there. They were angry. 'Tell your followers to be quiet,' they hissed at Jesus.

Jesus shook his head. 'It won't help if they keep quiet,' he said.

It was quite clear that something important was going to happen. It was going to happen soon.

The rabbis are angry to hear the crowds say Jesus is a king

Jesus rides a donkey. It is a sign he is a man of peace

Cloaks

16 Trouble Ahead

The Pharisees and the teachers of the Law felt very uneasy. What was Jesus going to do next?

First, Jesus went to the Temple. There was a market in the courtyard. People had set up stalls and were selling things for the festival. They were even selling live animals and birds.

'This is meant to be a place for prayer!' cried Jesus. He tipped the stalls over and drove everyone out.

Angry stall holders

Doves

Jesus overturns the market stalls

Coins

That made the priests angry. They met with the teachers of the Law and began to talk about getting rid of Jesus.

Jesus still preached his message. One day, he was by the Temple.

'Beware of the teachers of the Law,' he warned people. 'They make a big show of being religious, but they don't take care of people who are in need.'

He looked round. People were bringing festival gifts to the Temple collection box. The coins of the wealthy jingled noisily.

Then a widow came along. She gave two small coins.

'See!' said Jesus. 'She's given everything she has. What the rich people give is spare to them. Now she has nothing to live on.'

The religious leaders did not like being criticized. Then, at last, they got the chance they wanted. One of Jesus' disciples, Judas Iscariot, offered to help them catch Jesus. They paid him for his help.

Judas meets a rabbi in secret and tells him where to find Jesus

Rabbi

Judas Iscariot

17 The Last Supper

Jesus shares the cup of wine

Jesus breaks the bread

Jesus' followers meet for a special meal

The Passover meal was an important part of the Passover festival.

As people ate the special foods and said the special prayers, they remembered the promise God had made in the time of Moses, long ago:

'Keep my laws: then I will be your God and you will be my people.'

On the big day, Jesus asked his disciples to prepare a room where they could eat the Passover meal.

They gathered there in the evening.

During the meal, Jesus took a piece of bread, said a prayer of thanks, broke it, and gave it to his disciples. 'Take and eat it,' he said. 'This is my body.'

Then he took a cup of wine, said a prayer of thanks, and gave them the cup. 'Drink it, all of you,' he said. 'This is my blood.'

He tried to explain: his body was going to be broken; his blood was going to be shed; in this way, God would make a new promise to people.

The disciples didn't really understand. Everything at the meal went on as usual.

Except for one thing: Judas Iscariot slipped away.

A CHRISTIAN CEREMONY

The ceremony that Jesus carried out still happens when Christians meet as a church. The ceremony is often called Holy Communion. It is a time to remember Jesus' words and God's promise.

Judas Iscariot leaves the party

18 The Saddest Day

After the meal, Jesus and his disciples went out of the city. They went to an olive grove to sleep.

Jesus stayed awake and prayed to God. He knew there was trouble ahead.

A dark night in the olive grove called Gethsemane

Judas leads the armed men

Jesus prays

Then Judas Iscariot came back. He led a crowd of armed men. They marched Jesus off to the priests.

The disciples ran away.

In the morning, the religious leaders took Jesus to the Roman governor of Jerusalem: Pontius Pilate. 'He claims to be king of the Jews,' they said. 'That makes him a rebel. That means he deserves to die.'

After much arguing, they got their way.

Pilate's soldiers took Jesus to be punished.

They beat him and bullied him. Then they led him outside the city and crucified him.

Just before the sun went down, one of Jesus' followers came to take the body.

A few friends came to watch as the body was put in a stone tomb. The stone door was rolled shut.

Crucifixion is being nailed
to a cross of wood

GOOD FRIDAY

Christians remember Jesus' crucifixion on Good Friday – 'God's Friday'. They say prayers as they remember Jesus suffering; they say prayers asking God to help anyone who suffers.

A tomb with a
round stone door

19 Alive!

The day after Jesus was crucified was the sabbath, the Jewish day of rest.

Very early on the morning after that, some women went back to the tomb to say a last goodbye.

To their dismay, the door was open. The body had gone.

They saw angels. 'Why are you looking in a tomb for someone who is alive?' asked the angels. The women went to tell the disciples, but none of them really knew what to think.

Mary Magdalene went to the tomb and stayed there weeping. She saw someone, and thought it was the gardener.

It was Jesus.

Mary Magdalene sees the risen Jesus

Two friends recognize the risen Jesus

Two of Jesus' followers decided to walk home, a short way from Jerusalem. A man who was going the same way came along. They all talked about the happenings of the last few days – Jesus' crucifixion and the rumours that he was alive again. When the two followers reached their house, they invited the man to stay.

As he broke the bread they saw the man was Jesus. At once, he was gone.

The two hurried back to Jerusalem to tell the other disciples. As they were telling their story, Jesus appeared. He showed them his hands and feet: the marks of the crucifixion nails were clear.

Jesus' followers all believed one thing: Jesus was alive!

EASTER

Christians remember Jesus' resurrection on Easter Day. They even meet at sunrise to remember the joyful news about his new life.

20 A Message for the World

The risen Jesus spent time with his followers.

He explained that everything that had happened was part of God's plan.

He had told people of God's forgiveness; he had shown people the power of God's love.

'Now you must take the message I have preached to all the world,' he said. 'But wait: you will know when God gives you power to help.'

Not long after, the disciples saw Jesus being taken up to heaven. The disciples stayed in hiding. It was time for the festival of Pentecost, and they were

Jesus' followers receive the Holy Spirit

still in hiding in Jerusalem.

Then they heard a wind blowing. They saw flames reaching out and touching each of them.

They felt that God was with them. They felt bold enough to tell the world about Jesus. They proclaimed that he was God's promised king: the messiah, the Christ.

They went out to tell the world about God's forgiveness and God's love.

They went to tell everyone how to be part of God's kingdom.

PENTECOST

Christians celebrate Pentecost as the time when God's Holy Spirit came to help the disciples. They believe God's Holy Spirit helps all those who trust in Jesus.

Index